Black Butterflies
Selected Poems by Ingrid J[

Black Butterflies

Selected Poems by
Ingrid Jonker

Translated from Afrikaans by
André Brink and Antjie Krog

Human & Rousseau

Copyright in translations © André Brink and Antjie Krog

All rights reserved
Copyright © 2007 Ingrid Jonker Trust
First published in 2007 by Human & Rousseau,
An imprint of NB Publishers a division of Media24 Boeke (Pty) Ltd,
40 Heerengracht, Cape Town, 8001
Photo on cover: Desmond Windell
Cover design by Etienne van Duyker
Set in 10 on 14 pt New Baskerville by Alinea Studio, Kaapstad
Printed and bound by Novus Print Solutions, South Africa

First editon, first impressions 2007
Second impression 2007

ISBN: 978-0-7981-4892-4

First print-on-demand edition, first impression 2014
Third impression 2018
Printed and bound by CTP Printers, Cape Town

No part of this book may be reproduced or transmitted
in any form or by any electronic or mechanical means,
including photocopying and recording, or by any other
information storage or retrieval system, without written
permission from the publisher

Contents

Introduction 9

Escape

Escape 39
Puberty 40
At the Goodwood show 41
Song of the rag doll 42
Double game 43
Dedication 44
Wind song 45

Smoke and Ochre

1
On all faces 51
Pregnant woman 52
I repeat you 54
I went to seek for the path of my body 55
Autumn morning 56
I searched for my own heart 57
Forlorn city 58
Reclaimed land 59

2 *Intimate Conversation*
Don't sleep 63
When you call me 63
I know 63
When you laugh 63
When you were a baby 64

When you sleep   64
Your body   64
Every man has a head   64

3

Last night   67
The troubadour's ditty   68
Ramkiekie tune   69
Bitter-berry daybreak   70
You have tricked me   71
It's six of one   72
All too human   73
On the footpath   74

4

Early summer   77
Pixie love   78
Little grain of sand   79
Hush now the darkling man   80
Ladybird   81
My doll falls and breaks   82

5

The child who was shot dead by soldiers in Nyanga   85
On the death of a virgin   86
Seen from the wound in my side   87
I do not want to receive any more visits   88
Bushveld   89
25 December 1960   90
The song of the broken reeds   91
Daisies in Namaqualand   92
We   93
L'art poétique   94

Tilting Sun

Face of love   97
There's only one for ever   98
Tokoloshe   99
O the half-moon   100
Song of the grave digger   101
Conversation on a hotel terrace   102
Drawing   103
Walk   104
Dark stream   105
On the road to death   106
Dog   107
I lament you   108
The morning is you   109
Old man travelling   110
Two hearts   111
How long will it last   112
All that breaks   113
My embrace redoubled me   114
Lullaby for the beloved   115
When you write again   116
Waiting in Amsterdam   117
Journey around the world for André   118
Your name has a dinky car   119
Nostalgia for Cape Town   120
Plant me a tree André   121
This journey   122
Mommy   123
Waterfall of moss and sun   124
I am with those   125
I drift in the wind   126

Introduction

1. The Woman

I met Ingrid Jonker in the Green Point home of the author Jan Rabie and his painter wife Marjorie Wallace in the late afternoon of a blue-and-golden late-summer's day, Thursday 15 April 1963. There was a gathering of writers to plan a concerted protest against the new censorship bill which was taking shape in Parliament. Several of us had already launched individual attacks on the proposed onslaught on literature (sponsored by a prominent right-wing parliamentarian, Abraham Jonker, whose own forays into realist fiction had failed to live up to their initial promise), but it was now time for organised resistance on a larger scale. The discussion was energetic and passionate, but there was nothing yet to mark the day as exceptional. And then she came in, small and quiet but tense like a coiled spring, her curly hair unruly, her dark eyes guarded but smouldering. The daughter of the would-be Chief Censor, Abraham Jonker. She was wearing tight-fitting green pants. She was smoking. Her bare feet were small and narrow and beautiful. And within a few hours the course of my life was changed utterly.

In the course of that weekend I saw her eyes move through an amazing range of expressions, from cool and objective to flashing with ferocity, from serene to exuberant to apathetic to disillusioned to eager, from brazenly challenging and defiant to outraged to contemptuous, from widening with childlike wonder to burning with passion, from quietly content to scathing and vicious. And her sensitive, sensuous mouth: cynical, content, angry, vulnerable, playful, bitter, mocking, tranquil, furious, happy, generous, wild. Unpredictable and endlessly fascinating, those quicksilvery changes of mood and expression.

It was love at first sight, for both of us – even though I was married and she had been, for several years already, in an on-off relationship with the writer Jack Cope, twenty-odd years older than the two of us. As the French expression has it, we had been struck by lightning; and there was no holding back, as if we were already living under the cloud of apocalypse.

Even in the course of that first tumultuous weekend, before I had to return to Grahamstown where I was a lecturer in Afrikaans at Rhodes University, our near-interminable conversations introduced me to the landscapes of her life – often in brief, cryptic, unsettling flashes of almost blinding intensity; sometimes in longer, sustained journeys of discovery.

Ingrid was born on 19 September 1933 (there was some confusion about the date) on the farm of her maternal grandfather Fanie Cilliers, near the small North-Western Cape town of Douglas, close to the confluence of the Vaal and Orange River. (Having myself spent much of my youth in Douglas, the coincidence added to our sense of mutual recognition.) In one of her earliest photographs, one she remained particularly fond of, she stands naked on the edge of the water, a tiny nymph escaped from another world, scowling defiantly at the camera.

Her mother, Beatrice, had recently been abandoned by Abraham Jonker, who had cruelly accused her of carrying another man's child (possibly to shield his own marital infidelities). In due course he remarried twice and eventually started a new family in Cape Town with a writer of juvenile fiction, Lulu Brewis. Beatrice remained ailing for several years: leukemia, and a nervous condition which was to deteriorate so drastically that in the end she had to be taken away to the mental institution of Valkenburg, where she was confined more than once. ('I saw my mother going mad in front of my eyes,' Ingrid told me many times.)

After the grandfather's death in 1938 Beatrice, her mother and the two daughters (Ingrid and her older sister, Anna, born two years before her) moved to Durbanville, near Cape Town, where they lived in 'the house with the pepper tree';

and from there to Somerset West and Gordon's Bay, where Ingrid was to spend most of her early childhood. The girls played on the beach and in the sea like two small otters, or buried themselves in the fantasy world of books, or spent hours gathering and then hiding 'secrets' in the pine forest. These hidden or buried secrets became an indispensable part of Ingrid's life – not just as a treasure trove, but as a repository for memories, a self-made subconscious to the ordinary world. (Many years later, she would refer to a lover's sperm as 'secrets' too, as traces of a hidden space all her own.) And the sea became the background music to her poetry. She was passionate about it and could swim like a fish. And yet there is often an ominous undertone – or undertow – to it. As a small girl, even before she moved to Gordon's Bay, Ingrid had two frightening experiences of nearly drowning – once in a river, once in a dam. This, in a strange but significant way, linked in her mind the forces of life and death. And over the years all of it would find expression in her poetry.

The childhood world beside the sea brought the girls such bliss that they were hardly aware of the dire poverty in which their mother and grandmother had to eke out an existence. On many days there was only soup or fish-heads to eat; and when there was nothing at all, the fervent faith of the grandmother, *Ouma*, saw them through. She used to preach to the 'coloured' fishermen's families on Sundays, which provided Ingrid with an early inspiration for writing doggerel with a determined religious slant. Throughout her life the Bible remained a major framework of reference for her writing, not only in content but even more so in her choice of words, imagery, style. It provided the dark and the light, the dread and the exultation, the fear of hell and the expectation of heaven, as an answer to Ingrid's need to find a mythology of her own. And where the Bible ended, Ouma's elaborate commentaries, in the form of Thoughts for Every Day, took over. Often, while we were together, Ingrid would take out Ouma's *Thoughts* and read from the small blue pages covered in meticulous handwriting, collapsing in laughter as she adopted the declamatory voice of a *dominee*, but not really irreverently; religion became even more important to her after she had broken away from all organised forms of it.

In 1944 Beatrice died of cancer. Death had first invaded Ingrid's world when her grandfather passed away. Only a year after her mother, her beloved grandmother also died. This placed a barrier between the young girl and all her most precious memories of an edenic youth. From now on death would be a dark subtext to almost everything she wrote, but often in very ambiguous terms: whether as a consummation devoutly to be wished, or as a fearsome, threatening presence, as friend or dreaded enemy, as darkness or ultimate light.

Abraham returned out of the blue to reclaim his daughters. He did his best to integrate them into his new family (he soon had two new children with Lulu Brewis) and sent them to good schools; but Ingrid continued to feel neglected, and in later years complained (perhaps with some exaggeration) that she'd been made to work like a Cinderella for a stern and forbidding stepmother. Whatever happened on the surface of her life, she found more and more of a refuge in writing poetry, encouraged by a sympathetic teacher; and before she turned sixteen she had written most of the poems subsequently published in *Ontvlugting (Escape)*, 1956.

The small volume was dedicated to Ingrid's father, whose reaction was: 'My child, I hope there's more to it than the covers. I'll look at it tonight to see how you have disgraced me.'

In the meantime, at the end of 1951, Ingrid had completed her schooling with a not very impressive D aggregate – but with an A in Afrikaans. She was eager to go to university, but neither father Abraham nor stepmother Lulu would hear of it. She could enrol for a secretarial course to qualify herself for a job, but that was that. 'If you are old enough to write, you're mature enough to fend for yourself,' said Abraham, prompted by his wife. And so Ingrid moved out of the parental home ('There's space in the house, but not in the heart,' she explained curtly), and moved into a flat near the city centre, where for three years she did proofreading and copy-editing for various printers and publishers.

Her life entered a new phase in 1954 when she met Piet Venter, seventeen years older than herself, with two failed marriages behind him; a businessman with ambitions to become a writer. And two years later, soon after the publication of *Ontvlugting* they were married – which was more her decision than his. One of her long-cherished dreams, to have a child, now came within reach. (Even though an illogical fear of a miscarriage cast a pall over that eager expectation, as witness one of her best-known poems, 'Pregnant woman', which dates from 1957, the year of her pregnancy.) Ingrid had just moved into a very special cosmopolitan circle of creative artists among whom Piet, in spite of his ambitions, or perhaps because of them, felt sadly out of his depth. Among these friends were Jan Rabie, who had recently returned from a seven-year stay in Paris, and his Scottish wife Marjorie Wallace, the painters Erik Laubscher and his French wife Claude Bouscharain and the young art student Breyten Breytenbach, with the renowned bohemian poet and world traveller Uys Krige as *primus inter pares*. Through Uys, she would soon meet his close friend Jack Cope as well, with whom Uys shared a bungalow on Second Beach at Clifton. This circle transcended all the boundaries and taboos of the then newly established apartheid state, by including a number of 'coloured' poets and writers as well: Piet Philander, Richard Rive, Peter Clarke, Kenny Parker, Adam Small . . .

The birth of her daughter, Simone, was a watershed. The fulfilment of motherhood was accompanied by a discovery which Ingrid confided to me many years later: that on the day she returned home from hospital, she surprised Piet in bed with another woman. And less than eighteen months later the company he worked for transferred him to Johannesburg, which Ingrid was to describe as 'probably the most primitive city in the world', and which, moreover, meant leaving behind all the friends who had come to define her world. Whether there was any direct link or not, it comes as no surprise, with hindsight, that an early attempt at suicide dates from this period. (But to place it in perspective, one should bear in mind a memory evoked by Marjorie Wallace: that on the very first day she met Ingrid, the fledgling poet interrupted a carefree, happy conversation on Clifton beach by asking totally out of the blue, 'Do you think I will commit suicide one day?' Which was one of the key questions she also asked me during our first weekend together.)

'We miss the sound of the sea, and of course everything,' she wrote to Jack within her very first days in the north, '. . . the first 2 Johannesburg men I met on arrival were ugly fat and start drinking from 8 in the morning . . . I'm sorry my letter is so boring – there's nothing I can tell which I can say – I am so "robbed"!'

One of her earliest experiences in the then Transvaal was attending a cultural gathering, part of countrywide celebrations of the Afrikaans language, addressed by the infamous 'architect of apartheid', Dr Hendrik Frensch Verwoerd (whom she classified among the 'animals'): 'One form of verbal violence after the other occurred without a blush, until at last the seducer of our nation smugly sat down to the applause of White Afrikanerdom.'

There were a few luminous moments amid the gloom, one of which was meeting the playwright and publisher Bartho Smit, who later published her seminal volume of poetry *Rook en Oker* (*Smoke and Ochre*) 1963, and his actress wife, Kita Redelinghuys. But in most respects the sojourn in Johannesburg was disastrous. Within three months Ingrid fled back to the Cape, without any luggage and without Simone.

Piet Venter soon followed her to take her 'home', but for all practical purposes the marriage was over; and from this time the relationship with Jack Cope became serious – even though he tried to keep her at a distance by warning her that he was 'just like an old broken reed'. In a letter to Uys Krige, written at about the same time, Ingrid manipulates the exchange by telling her father-mentor-friend that what Jack had written to her was: 'Uys thinks you're a broken reed.' Whatever the correct version, it found its way into the moving poem, 'The song of the broken reeds.'

Moving into the more lively, colourful, cosmopolitan suburb of Hillbrow in Johannesburg made life more bearable for Ingrid; but not for long. Early in 1960 she finally left Piet and returned to Cape Town, this time taking Simone with her. (The divorce was finalised in early 1962.) It came at a critical moment in the country's history, unleashed by the massacre at Sharpeville on 21 March 1960. Violence erupted all over South Africa. In Cape Town, among other shocking incidents, a black baby was shot dead in his mother's arms by police in the black township of Nyanga. Driven by outrage and morbid fascination, Ingrid went to the police station at Philippi to see the body. And in a single burst of inspiration she wrote what Uys Krige termed one of the very best poems in free verse in our literature, 'The child shot dead by soldiers at Nyanga'. Apart from bowing to pressure to shorten the title of the poem to 'The Child', she refused to change a word, and like the baby she addressed in it, the poem has since travelled the world in many languages, finding its ultimate niche in President Nelson Mandela's speech at the opening of the first democratically elected Parliament in South Africa, in May 1994. 'I am surprised when people call it political,' Ingrid wrote in an article in *Drum* (May, 1963). 'It grew out of my own experiences and sense of bereavement. It rests on a foundation of all philosophy, a certain belief in "life eternal", a belief that nothing is ever wholly lost.'

In other respects, too, those years were difficult for Ingrid. The relationship with Jack offered her a sense of security, although its open-endedness was a source of frustration and friction; a nadir was reached when she discovered, in the middle of 1961, that she was pregnant. She postponed telling Jack

15

for two months; when she finally mustered the courage to inform him, his only reaction, as she told me two years later, was to ask, 'What are you going to do about it?' As to what she did, accounts differ. Her sister Anna, over-anxious to cover up, reported that Ingrid had checked herself into a hospital. Ingrid herself maintained, in gory detail, that it was a backstreet affair, performed by an old 'coloured' woman armed with a knitting needle. The brush with death intrinsic to the experience found expression in another of her best-known poems, 'Little grain of sand'. It was one of the most traumatic moments of her life, which continued to haunt her till the end. And although the relationship with Jack resumed, it could never be the same again.

What particularly distressed Ingrid was remembering her mother who, when abandoned thirty years earlier by Abraham Jonker during her pregnancy, had chosen, nevertheless, in dire circumstances, to keep her baby. That Beatrice, who had had much more reason for an abortion, had decided against it, caused Ingrid guilt feelings of which she could never rid herself. Often, in moments of high tension, she would confuse herself, the child who had survived, with the foetus she had aborted. No wonder that in the period following the abortion she had to be hospitalised more than once in the Valkenburg mental institution, where among other forms of treatment she was also submitted to electric shock therapy. And inevitably her fixation on suicide became near-pathological.

These dark years – the final months in Johannesburg, the return to the Cape – resulted in heightened poetic activity. For quite some time Ingrid had been working on a new volume, but it was twice turned down by one of the foremost Afrikaans poets, Dirk Opperman, who was also a reader for a publisher. Much of the verse in *Ontvlugting* had been modelled on Opperman's characteristic mastery of the rhymed couplet, which persisted in her work for a long time; but gradually, notably under the influence of Uys Krige and his magnificent translations of Éluard, Lorca, Neruda and other Latin poets, she turned to free verse. And soon she had a collection of poems that was destined to become the cornerstone of her oeuvre, *Rook en Oker* (*Smoke and Ochre*), published in October 1963 by Bartho Smit at APB Publishers in Johannesburg. The splendid cover was designed by a young Cape artist, Nico Hagen.

During that first weekend I spent in the small Bantry Bay apartment which Ingrid shared with a good friend, Lena Oelofse, Nico turned up late one afternoon, with a nervous young woman in tow. He had come, he announced, to inform Ingrid of his wedding earlier that same day. She was speechless with shock. It transpired that during a lull in her relationship with Jack she had been having an affair with Nico and that he had already proposed marriage to her.

'We would love to have you as a friend,' he assured her.

'Fuck your friendship!' Ingrid responded in rage. 'Get the hell out of here, you bloody traitor!'

She promptly withdrew into the warm amniotic water of a bath, where she sat for an hour in total silence, smoking one cigarette after the other. We had already arranged to go out for a meal, but it was almost impossible to extricate her from the bath. In the end she agreed to go with me – not to eat, but to drink. 'I want to get drunk tonight,' she said laconically.

Outside the restaurant she collapsed in tears. When at last she became calmer, she started talking compulsively. Why had Nico done such a thing to her? And he wasn't the only one. *Everybody* took advantage of her, used her, abused her. What was wrong with her? Because, surely, it was all her own fault . . .

It took a long time before we went inside. Over the meal – she did consent to eat something, in the end – she told me the whole convoluted story of her life and loves. Time and time again she returned to Simone, who was with Piet Venter in Johannesburg at the time. 'They're going to take away my child. And the court will side with them. Because I take drugs. I drink. I sleep around. But I *want* my child!' And inevitably, like many times during that weekend, she spoke of suicide. She showed me the thin white scars on her wrists from a previous attempt. Yet when I left very early on the Monday morning to drive home the nearly one thousand kilometres to Grahamstown, there was something incredibly serene and almost happy in the smile with which she said good-bye.

We had both assumed that the weekend would remain outside of time, outside of our ordinary lives; we never believed it would continue. But within a week everything had changed. We both realised that we were too deeply in love to extricate ourselves. I received an invitation to return to Cape Town at the end of May. For her, this seemed to be an unexpected new lease on life. At the same time my appearance on the scene had rekindled Jack's passionate interest.

For the rest of the year, unable to stay away, I drove down to Cape Town every few weeks. Ingrid had become a fever in the blood. When we were together, the ordinary flow of life stopped; time no longer existed. We would spend the weekends in romantic hideouts: country hotels near Stellenbosch, Franschhoek, Gordon's Bay. She was swept along on a new wave of writing poetry; even I began to write poems – very bad ones, terribly derivative, but I needed the outlet. Our love became an extension of our creative writing, as our writing flowed from the agonies and ecstasies of love. But very soon a fatal pattern was established: I would rush down to Cape Town in a frenzy of longing and desire, only to find, within a day or two, that in my absence she had been with Jack again – sometimes because he would not leave her in peace, just as often because *she* could not bear to be alone. This would inhibit my urge for commitment (what Ingrid wanted above all, was to get married), and I would become serious about returning to Grahamstown and my marriage. And of course this decision would then persuade Ingrid to turn to Jack again – by which time, back at the ranch, I would decide that my marriage had failed after all, and I would rush back, head over heels, to Cape Town, only to find that in my absence . . . et cetera.

Time and time again we would break up, sometimes with a whimper, often with a bang. Time and time again we would dive back into the love which beckoned like a dark and dangerous current. It could not possibly last.

Early in 1964 Ingrid was awarded the biggest literary prize in South Africa at the time for *Rook en Oker*. She decided that she would use the money to go to Europe, where she had never been, possibly to study in Holland. (The first person she telephoned with the news of the prize, offering to pay for his air ticket to the awards ceremony in Johannesburg, was Abraham Jonker. He declined.) We agreed that as soon as possible I would follow. I would take her to Paris, the city I loved more than any other; afterwards we would travel through Spain. (The publishing firm of Human & Rousseau had commissioned me to do a travel book, and paid an advance to finance the trip.) Our travel plans had to be kept secret, of course: Jack was not to know; and my marriage was still precariously surviving.

At the end of March Ingrid left Cape Town for Southampton on the *Windsor Castle*. Almost every day she wrote letters to her two lovers left behind. She also met the writer Laurens van der Post, something of a legend (largely self-consciously created) in his lifetime. He became her new mentor and undertook to introduce her to the literary world in London. At the same time it was clear from Ingrid's letters that, if van der Post's attitude was, above all, fatherly, it was not without incestuous undertones. In Britain at least one other South African writer in exile, David Lytton, came under her spell. (When she turned down his amorous invitations, he assured her that, 'Now you have missed your chance with one of the lords of life.')

The six weeks in Britain were both exhilarating and bewildering; she never quite felt at ease, and her nostalgia for

South Africa became worse. (Even more so because of the absence of Dylan Thomas, with whose poetry she had become infatuated.) When she moved to Amsterdam, the sense of *dépaysement* increased. A particular source of distress was that her room had no mirror in it. Ingrid had always been obsessed with mirrors, with the need to see herself reflected. There was nothing narcissistic about it, and no vanity at all: what she needed, more and more, was the constant reassurance that *she was there*. As her confidence ebbed, this need became almost pathological.

The stay in Amsterdam – relieved indeed by meeting some Dutch writers and poets to whom Jan Rabie and others had provided her with introductions – became, in her own words, 'a waking nightmare'. The most memorable poem ringing out like a *vox clamantis* from this darkness, was 'Waiting in Amsterdam', based on a dream about my imminent arrival. She copied it out for Jack, dedicated to him; with another copy for me, dedicated accordingly.

On Saturday 20 June I arrived in Amsterdam – to find that, instead of the secrecy we had planned for the visit, Ingrid had already arranged radio interviews for us (jointly and severally) and had thoroughly briefed everybody at the NZAV (the Dutch-South Africa Society) about our impending 'honeymoon'. This, linked to her insistence that we dine at the most expensive restaurants and live it up as much as possible, together with the almost unbearably high expectations we had both brought to the visit, created tensions from the first hour. These were carried over to Paris, where we lodged in a seedy but charming little hotel on the Rue Monsieur le Prince, off the Boulevard Saint Michel. But the tensions were temporarily held in check by the magic of Paris itself and by meetings with outlandish and stimulating people, most notably the exiled poet-painter Breyten Breytenbach, who was an old friend of Ingrid's and with whom I'd been corresponding for a long time although we'd never met. (Breyten had by then married the lovely Vietnamese Yolande, a union regarded as 'immoral' in terms of South African legislation, which meant that he could not return to his country.) There were magical nights at the Coupole or the Sélect or on the Place Saint-Sulpice, or up on Montmartre, or along the banks of the Seine. But there were also eruptions of temper, recriminations, shouting, tears. (One of the most amazing discoveries I made about Ingrid was her ability to turn away from the most explosive quarrels and quietly sit down to write some of her most serenely beautiful lines; sometime during our few days in the Rue Monsieur le Prince she composed 'Journey Around the World'.)

And then came Spain, which was to be the culmination of our trip. Before we could rent a car to embark on the long planned journey, I had to spend several days in Barcelona meeting publishers to arrange options on children's books for my Cape Town publisher: this had been part of the justification for the advance Human & Rousseau had paid me. But Ingrid refused to be left alone in the hotel, and was too scared to venture out on her own. I reasoned, argued, pleaded. To which she would respond by trying to seduce me, at first subtly, then blatantly, into staying. But in the end, hyperconscious of my obligations to the publishers who had made the trip possible, I had no choice but to go ahead, making appointments and keeping them. On my return the door would be locked. If I insisted, she would start screaming so loudly that people came running to see who was being assaulted or murdered. Eventually we would gloriously make up. But within an hour the whole exercise would be repeated, each time with more sound and fury. Even the management, undoubtedly accustomed to the legendary *furia español*, became concerned. Our whole relationship turned destructive, self-destructive. And ahead of me, always, loomed the obligation of the journey and the book I had been commissioned to write on it.

The end was inevitable. There were a few happier interludes, including an afternoon at a corrida. But our time in the light was over. For us, already darkness was, like Cummings's snow, carefully, everywhere, descending.

In a moment of quiet despair we both agreed that it would be better for her to return to Paris, where Breyten and Yolande could take care of her, and where, we both hoped, she could still turn her holiday into something rewarding. Breyten was informed by telegram. The next day we set out for the airport. Ingrid was abnormally subdued. When her flight was called she suddenly became hysterical and refused to go to the gate, throwing such a tantrum that half of the airport officials came running to add to the commotion. In the end a doctor was called, who gave her an injection. And we returned to the hotel, dispirited and resentful.

The following day, with due warning to Breyten, the whole scene was repeated, this time in a minor key and without histrionics. Ingrid flew to Paris, and I set out for a month's exploration of Spain. (In the very first card she sent me from Paris, on the evening of her return, she quoted D. H. Lawrence, equating in her mind the bullfight with love: 'You have got to be good . . . if you are not good your love is a mess and your courage a slaughter.') It was only at the very end of the holiday that I learned, with shock, in a letter from my publisher, that Ingrid had in fact returned to Cape Town.

It was not until much later that the details were filled in. How her mental state in Paris had deteriorated so suddenly that Breyten had to arrange for her to be hospitalised in the institution of Sainte Anne; how through the intervention of Roy MacNab, cultural attaché at the South African Embassy, she had been released and put on a plane. She also revealed that Jack wanted nothing more to do with her; and – the only ray of light – that her period had arrived on time, which meant that she was not pregnant as we had feared.

It should have been the end, but it wasn't. Within a month or two our correspondence resumed in all its intensity. Moments of disillusionment and rebellion were swept away by rekindled passion. Early in December I was back in Cape Town.

On the surface everything returned to what had been

before. Yet not really. Something had been lost; there was a touch of urgency, an almost frantic need to reassure ourselves that all was still well. But we both knew, and in vulnerable moments acknowledged, that our love could no longer be what it had been. For Ingrid the pain was almost unbearable; it implied a loss of that surprising innocence, that child-like quality, as of an elf or a sprite, which should remain forever untouched by the pettiness of the ordinary world.

One particularly stormy episode still haunts my memory: it was a night in December; I was to drive home to Grahamstown very early the next morning. An argument arose. It became unbearable. Near midnight, beside herself with rage, Ingrid ran out of the apartment (she was by then living in an ugly modern block, *Bonne Esperance*, on the beachfront where Three Anchor Bay merges into Sea Point) screaming that she was going to kill herself. By this time I was so tired, and had heard the threat so many times, that I did not believe it. But an hour later a stranger brought her back to the door: she had tried to jump in front of his car. We were both in shock. For hours we talked, and cried, and slowly found our way back, as always, to caring and forgiveness and love. And then, exhausted, I went to sleep. Ingrid stayed awake, and on the narrow porch outside the room, with her small writing pad on her lap, wrote the moving poem 'Plant me a tree André'.

For some time we kept the embers alive, mainly by working together very closely on the polishing of my experimental novel *Orgie*, based on our love and on Ingrid's life. It had been scheduled for publication the year before, but political intervention had forced Bartho Smit to cancel the project. Now a new publisher, John Malherbe, was going to bring it out in a particularly beautiful publication in March of 1965. I returned to Cape Town, and together we celebrated the occasion, not realising that it was to be our final farewell. (A week or so later there was a note from her to confirm the arrival of her period: once again there was to be 'no butterfly'. Over the previous two years there had always been a particular poignancy about those notes, a sense of loss and emptiness, each time a new farewell, a different kind of failure, another small death.)

By that time she had already met the Flemish painter Herman van Nazareth, who was to become (or had already become) one of her last lovers. She had spoken of him in glowing terms. Perhaps I should have sensed something, but I did not. Soon after my departure I, too, met someone else, in Pretoria. And fell in love, and decided to marry. Looking back now, forty years later, it is pretty evident that I was desperate to clutch at the first straw to extricate myself from a relationship which had become impossible to handle, and from a marriage that had by then irreparably broken down.

At the end of April, almost two years to the day since our first meeting, I wrote to tell Ingrid about it. We had one last telephone conversation. Her reaction was very similar to the one with which in that first of our cruellest months she had thrown Nico Hagen out. There are confusing and conflicting reports about the last few months. About several heady affairs, surrounding the central relationship with the painter. About one or more abortions. About ruptures with friends. About an accident in which she broke her leg. About terrible financial straits.

On Monday 19 July 1965, on a visit to Pretoria, I received a telephone call from a close friend, the author Abraham de Vries, to tell me that Ingrid had committed suicide by walking into the sea a hundred metres from her apartment. (Ingrid, who could swim like a fish . . .!) Her body, as she had predicted in poems written since before her sixteenth birthday, and reiterated in several recent letters and telephone calls to friends, diary entries, jottings on odd scraps of paper, had been found 'washed ashore in weeds and grass'.

However predictable it seemed in retrospect, when it happened it was unbearable, and unbelievable. I felt the world grow dark in front of my eyes. For the rest of the day I was blind and could not see.

It was almost unbearable to resist the impulse to travel to Cape Town for the funeral; but the idea of facing the world of prying strangers, the knowing eyes of friends and acquaintances, facing Jack, facing the press, was just too much. I could not turn my grief into a public performance; it was too private and too deep. And so I missed the ultimate spectacle of her funeral, where the dour members of the Jonker family, protected by Security Police, glowered across the grave at the special friends – writers and artists – gathered on the other side; missed the spectacle of Jack trying to hurl himself onto the coffin; missed, too, the second funeral, a week later, when the real friends met at the grave again to read from Ingrid's work.

And now, I suppose, she belongs to the ages. Quite an industry has sprung up around her life and death. This volume is an attempt to get past the many accretions to her story, to the essence of her legacy: the poetry.

2. The Poet

Ingrid's first volume, *Escape* (1956), did not attract much attention, and it was not difficult to see why. The reviews were never scathing, but were marked, mostly, by condescending kindness. Yet, in the light of the work that was to follow, it becomes clear that the best of even those early poems were more than just 'charming', 'pleasing', or 'promising', those damning words of faint praise. Much of it is typical of adolescence, the self-centred, exquisite sufferings of first love, rejection or doubt; the nostalgia for passing or lost innocence; the child-like wonder at the incomprehensible complexities of the world.

But knowing where she came from, and more especially where she was going to, one can recognise stirrings of a deeper anguish, an unusually dark awareness of the helplessness of the individual, particularly the child-woman on the threshold of maturity, in the face of indomitable forces and obstacles. Above all, there is an acknowledgement of the ubiquitous threat of death: sometimes it concerns the individual death (as in the surprising, even chilling, premonition of her own drowning in the title poem, 'Escape'); more often there is the awareness of death as fate, an inescapable dark undertone to life itself, in the image of the 'tokoloshe', the threatening troll-like creature from African mythology, or in the rag doll casually destroyed by its owner, the ultimate symbol of female helplessness ('Song of the rag doll'), or the apocalyptic vision which informs even small, seemingly casual poems.

There are many intimations of this lurking, unavoidable death: it need not always be invoked directly, but often speaks from irreparable loss ('Puberty'), suffering, loneliness or longing for the unattainable (of which the strong, almost hallucinatory image of the prize bull in 'At the Goodwood show' must rank as the most impressive), or in metaphors of spiritual death.

Death is not only contrasted with love as a live-giving and redemptive experience, but often coincides with it: the one becomes unthinkable without the other. Ultimately everything becomes a masquerade, a game in which one loses touch with reality. Occasionally there is a strongly religious hope of salvation in one form or another; but more often than not the prospect remains bleak and depressing. In the very moment of meeting between two lovers the heartbreak of the end is already present.

In one way or another most of these poems concern an underlying awareness of a relationship – between woman and man, child and parent, you and I, ego and alter ego: and from this 'double game' arises a persistent impression of a life left incomplete, broken, shattered, condemned forever to search for the magic word, or the magic potion, which may restore the lost wholeness of the primal couple.

Weaker poems are often saved by escaping from the adolescent sin of vagueness and generalisation through small evocative images or allusions which lend precision and definition to the lines: what prevents 'Escape' from sinking into sentimentality are the loaded connotations of Valkenburg (the place of darkness, of marginality, of madness, of rejection, informed by memories of her mother's experience, and unsettlingly prophetic of her own) and of Gordon's Bay, the name in which all the innocence and timeless bliss of childhood are encapsulated. Following from this opening couplet, small precise images continue to add to the sense of poetic density: the careless game with tadpoles in a stream evoking the grown-up world of sex, as yet undreamt of; the swastikas evoking a world at war beyond the Eden of childhood; the dog roaming the deserted beaches, the gull swooping down in search of food. Against this backdrop, even the somewhat pretentious penultimate couplet becomes digestible – especially when the vague notion of the fulfilment of grief finds expression in those lapidary concluding lines:

> *Washed out my body lies in weed and grass*
> *in all the places where we once did pass.*

The lyricism in this poetry is unmistakeable. The cadences of folk songs will continue to mark her work to the end. In 'Wind song' the apparent lightheartedness with which love and longing are evoked, really masks deep experiences of disillusionment and suffering – made bearable by the sheer musicality of the verse. Indeed, our sweetest songs are those that tell of saddest thought.

Ingrid seems to have been cannily aware of the youthful dangers of Weltschmerz and whimsicality, which may have been one reason for bracing the often rather limp emotions by a strong framework of rhyme and metre, probably influenced by her early Afrikaans model, Dirk Opperman. Of course this invites the risk of relying too much on what soon becomes purely external props; and often indeed, iambic monotony sets in, reinforced by the deadening predictability of rhyme. Yet in her better poems, even at such an early stage in her short career, these rhymes can be impressively functional: either by introducing a sound of inescapable fate, like a tolling bell, as a subtext to all human frivolity, or by lending force and confidence to what might otherwise all too readily lapse into aimless meandering.

The small circle of Ingrid's friends in Cape Town, especially those who knew of the hours and days she spent working on revision with Uys Krige, were aware of the remarkable new maturity in her work ever since her marriage and following her return to Cape Town; but to the literary public *Smoke and Ochre* (1963) came as a total surprise. With this single slim volume she placed herself among the foremost poets of Afrikaans; after her suicide in 1965 she acquired the status of an icon. Through her open rebellion against her father and all the values of the establishment he represented, and the romantic fascination of an entire young generation of readers with her death at such a young age, she became a figurehead – a female James Dean, a symbol of martyred yet triumphant femininity, like Sylvia Plath or Anne Sexton. To this day her work, and notably *Smoke and Ochre,* remains among the most popular setworks in Afrikaans literature at several universities.

There are occasional impulses from her early work still stirring in the new collection – a few persistent couplets and quatrains, particularly in the seemingly playful lyricism of the love poems in Part 3, where the influence of Opperman and an early generation of Afrikaans poets remains notable; but the full extent of her renewal is evident from her supple and supremely confident handling of free verse. Her enormous indebtedness to the French surrealist Paul Éluard, the romantic and elegiac figure of the Spanish Lorca, and South Americans like Neruda and Andrade, all of whom she had encountered through the masterly translations and illuminating commentaries of Uys Krige, is obvious from the very first of the opening poem, 'On all faces'. No longer bound to the formal exigencies of rhyme and metre, the rhythm of these poems is determined by units of imagery or thought impulses, conceived in musical terms (often enhanced, and visually dramatised, by the use of spacing within the separate lines).

If smoke may be said to represent dreams, air, the spirit, and ochre the substance of body and earth, the dimension in which these two meet and merge is love. It is indeed the key to the volume, and it is all the flickering facets and intimations of love which lend the collection its sense of endless variety. This often takes the form of a celebration of the fleeting instant, the French *instantané*, the perception of 'the lightness of your body in flight' ('I went to seek for the path of my body'), 'and your body that plunges into the wounded autumn' ('Autumn morning'), or the exquisite series of 'snapshots' of the lover in 'Intimate conversation' (all of them transplanted from Ingrid's only play, *A son after my own heart*, written for the actor Pietro Nolte in Johannesburg soon after her marriage, but never performed during her lifetime). Otherwise, there are the remarkable poems in which love becomes all-embracing, encompassing the whole world ('On all faces', 'Forlorn city', 'Reclaimed land') or integrating the 'I' with the whole of humanity ('It's six of one'), in the way the child shot dead at Nyanga becomes a giant striding through the world without a pass.

Love often brings with it disillusionment and loss ('You have tricked me'), but also a heightened awareness of the miraculous (as in the delicate lullabies written for Simone, like 'Early summer' or 'Pixie love'). If it regularly tends towards the lyrical, with melancholy undertones (notably in Part 3, culminating in the haunting 'Bitter-berry daybreak'), it can also slide into a deeper and darker awareness of death, as in the ironical evocations of abortion or miscarriage in 'Pregnant woman', the image of a falling doll in 'My doll falls and breaks', or even the poem 'We', in which the beginning of a new love already presages the end.

The body may be the site of love (one is often reminded of Donne's immortal homage, in 'The extasie', to our bodies which 'Did us to us at first convay'), but the body itself has no substance or being of its own: it is conditioned, and even shaped, by the presence and hands of the lover: '...my breasts/ which imitate the hollows of your hands' ('I repeat you').

The volume becomes a confession of faith in the simplest affirmations of life, as in the delicate 'Daisies in Namaqualand', or in the fine web of imagery which summarises her poetic credo ('Little grain of sand', or 'L'art poétique'). But among the most memorable of her poems in *Smoke and Ochre* are those from Part 5 where the quivering music of solo flute or violin or harpsichord which seems to characterise most of the love poetry gives way to an organ played at full throttle: 'The child', 'On the death of a virgin', 'Seen from the wound in my side', 'I do not want to receive any more visits' . . . Closest in tone to the South Americans whom she encountered through Uys Krige, the magnificent rhetoric and imagery of these poems have a visionary quality which stamp her authority on the literary landscape of South Africa.

A year after Ingrid's death, Jack Cope and her sister, Anna, compiled a posthumous collection published as *Kantelson* (*Tilting Sun*), 1966. It was not comprehensive, and there were some unacceptable editorial decisions, notably to excise two lines from 'Waiting in Amsterdam' ('you took off your cock/ laid it on the table') which Jack had regarded as distasteful and 'unpublishable' and Anna thought unworthy of Ingrid – even though, as it happened, they were the punch lines of the entire poem. (Following a public controversy, the lines were later reinstated in the Afrikaans *Collected Works,* although Anna perversely continued to argue that interpreting the lines as sexual was a misreading. The whole affair is a barometer of the devastating influence censorship was having on South African, and particularly Afrikaans, literature. Ingrid herself, it should be said, regarded the poem as very funny.)

The best poems in *Tilting Sun* beautifully complement those in *Smoke and Ochre*. Overall, as one might expect against the background of her last two years, the tone is darker, the disillusionment and even cynicism more marked. In response to an increasing sense of personal futility (as expressed in 'I lament you'), the anger about betrayal often overshadows other emotions – whether in the agonised warning of the beloved against appropriation by the arch-enemy, the bourgeoisie ('Your name has a dinky car'), or in the sneering rejection of the lover who is to be mourned with swallows under the armpits and a white cross, 'For the man/ of whom you once reminded me' ('This journey'); in the image of the lover who arrives after an interminable agony of waiting, only to unscrew his sex and abandon both her and the world ('Waiting in Amsterdam'), or in her fierce identification with the despised and rejected, against the values which no longer function in a post-lapsarian world – justice, which doesn't exist; brotherhood, which is a fraud; love, which has no right ('I am with those'), and most shockingly in her exultant identification with Judas Iscariot, the 'very verb of love' ('On the road to death').

One senses a growing desperation in her grasping for the redemptive power of love ('Face of love', 'There's only one for ever', 'O the half-moon', 'Drawing' . . .) because in the heart of love itself, which has been transformed into one of the manifestations of the evil tokoloshe (as in the eponymous poem, or in those others where love is no more than a temporary shelter for death: 'All that breaks', 'When you write again', etc).

There are still moments of serenity and grace, when hope breaks out of hopelessness ('Journey around the world', or 'Plant me a tree'), a cherishing of delightful small moments of fun and tenderness (as in 'Two hearts', or 'Lullaby for the beloved', and some others). But all too often she seems to have lost touch with life and with the world, as in the image of the woman (in the guise of both her own mother and of herself as the mother of Simone) who is no longer a human being, only 'an a'.

Underlying, in many different forms, the love poetry, one recognises again the decisive importance of experiencing almost everything within the framework of a relationship, an I and a you (even if these two are more dramatically than ever before out of step with each other). No wonder that the mirror remains a crucial image. On its own, the self is never adequate: only through being 'redoubled' by the image of the other, or by recognising in the other the face of the self, can there be any hope of salvation. But of course, since the other becomes ever less trustworthy, the self is also heading towards an ultimately inevitable disaster.

Because the poet had not been able to subject the poems to a final revision, and because, for the sake of inclusiveness, a number of early, unpublished poems were also included in the collection, *Tilting Sun*, as a whole, lacks the wholeness of *Smoke and Ochre*. But it does round off Ingrid Jonker's work in a way that comes to match, sometimes uncannily, the closure she herself chose to bring to her life.

3. The Translation

Following Mandela's highlighting of 'The Child' in his first speech to Parliament in 1994, there has been a steady increase in the level of interest in Ingrid Jonker's work, further stimulated by two television documentaries on her life and poetry in 2002. In Afrikaans, a number of highly talented and exciting younger musicians, most notably Chris Chameleon, began to turn Ingrids's poetry into songs that almost immediately became enormously popular. Internationally, this trend was also manifested in the Netherlands.

When Antjie Krog and I embarked on the project of translating Ingrid's poetry, the original intention was to establish a *Collected Poems* for an international audience. But precisely because it was aimed at such a wide readership, most of which was almost wholly unfamiliar with her writing, we believed that it would be doing an injustice to the perception of her work as a whole to include so many early (and even some later) poems of inferior quality, which relied heavily on the mechanics of rhyme and metre. At best, one knows from Cervantes, *any* translation is like viewing a tapestry from the reverse; but it is particularly true of poetry – and even more so of less dense poetry. At the same we hoped to ensure a translation fairly representative of the different kinds and phases of her work, which made it possible to err on the side of leniency in the selection.

An early edition of translations from her work, the *Selected Poems* produced by Jack Cope and William Plomer (first published by Heinemann; later revised and enlarged for a 1988 edition by Human & Rousseau, Cape Town) paved the way. But in spite of some sensitive and rewarding work, these translations were often unsatisfactory, Cope's knowledge of Afrikaans being, at best, shaky, and Plomer's by his own admission non-existent. And even the extended edition contained only forty-five poems, excluding some of the best and most characteristic of Ingrid's work.

The edition of her poetry we chose as the sourcebook for this translation is the reliable and in many respects remarkable collected works, the *Versamelde Werke* edited by Abraham H de Vries in 1984. Very rarely, and only when there were very good reasons, did we deviate from his text. A peculiar example is 'Waiting in Amsterdam' where we decided to combine the two separate dedications Ingrid used in the two first versions of the poem which she sent to her two different lovers.

Having made our initial selection, on the basis, not only of quality but of representativeness, Antjie Krog and I, with the editorial help of one of the finest English poets in South Africa, Ingrid de Kok, confronted the main task of translation. The basic choice was between an attempt to do justice primarily to the semantic level – the imagery, the flow of thought, the various strands of meaning – or to the external structure (which, obviously, in good poetry is never really 'external' or 'supplementary' at all) of rhyme and metre/rhythm which supports, reveals and enhances meaning. This concerned most particularly the early poems which rely so heavily for their effect on forms like rhyming couplets or quatrains. As far as possible, we tried to do justice to both these dimensions, but in several instances an 'either/or' approach simply did not work. Rather than making a final choice in terms of a volume (or section of a volume) as a whole, we preferred making ad hoc decisions concerning each separate poem. This means that in some cases, as in 'At the Goodwood show' where rhyme was vital to the whole, to reinforce in sound the bull's experience of being restrained and imprisoned, we tried to adhere as far as possible to the rhyming couplet scheme; while in others (like the bewitching 'Little grain of sand') we – reluctantly – opted for the flow of thought and imagery, introducing rhyme and/or metre only where these seemed to enter more or less naturally into this flow. Consequently, in several poems (for example, 'Escape', 'Puberty' and others from the first volume), we used rhyme in some of the couplets, and not in others. In such cases, where it did not seem possible to do justice to both, we had to choose between *meaning* (as in 'Double game') and rhyme and/or metre. We are aware of a certain stiltedness in a number of the translations, particularly of poems we believed *had* to be included to illustrate a certain tendency in her work, like the obsession with certain prophetic images of death and drowning; to omit them altogether would have diminished the overall impression.

In a way, but only in a way, it was 'easier' to deal with the free verse in *Smoke and Ochre* and *Tilting Sun*, but it is, of course, a form with an inner discipline which is often more rigorous than that of a prescribed metric scheme or rhyming pattern. In several poems where a choice of words (particularly verbs) or the contours of a phrase may appear unusual, this was done in an attempt to retain a comparable feature of the

Afrikaans text, more often than not inspired by Ingrid's models among the French or Spanish/South American surrealists (a good example is 'On all faces'). Even so, some of our solutions may still not be entirely convincing. But again, to omit the poems concerned, would have left lacunae too disturbing of the whole.

Occasionally, we decided to use Afrikaans words (especially in plant names like 'frutang' or 'moederkappie') or words coined by the poet for special effect ('appeliefkosie'): in each of these cases the term is explained at the bottom of the page.

In a few cases startlingly different versions of the same poem were available. 'Nostalgia for Cape Town' (included in *Tilted Sun*), for example, contained the line, 'She is my mother', for which was substituted, in the other, 'I am her enfant terrible': here we were forced to make a choice which seemed to fit better into the context; but readers may do well to keep the suppressed line at the back of their minds. In 'I drift in the wind' the last line refers, in one instance, to 'black butterflies', in the other to 'black crows': here our choice was motivated by an overview of Ingrid's poetry, in which 'butterflies' plays a more significant role; in the end it even prompted our choice of a title for the volume. In the same poem Ingrid's play on the subtle nuances of 'eensaam' and 'vereensaamd' prompted the use of both 'lonely' and the more American, but suggestive, 'lonesome'.

There is one poem which Ingrid did not write as poetry: it is 'How long will it last', first published in *Kantelson*. Originally it was the conclusion of one of the early letters she wrote to me, but divided into lines it seemed to be so 'poetic' that it was turned into a poem on her behalf.

Ingrid made translations of some of her own poems ('25 December 1960', 'With those', 'This journey'). Where feasible, we used these as the basis of our translation, with small modifications where her version in what, for her, was very much a second language, did not seem to do justice to the meaning of her own original Afrikaans.

In most cases, Antjie and I would each do our own translations of a poem, after which we would meet to discuss and hammer out a second draft; this would then be passed on to Ingrid de Kok for comment and recommendations, before all three of us would meet for prolonged sessions of mixing and matching, of trial and error, before arriving at something like consensus.

After the initial sponsor reneged on her commitments, there followed an interval of several years before Kerneels Breytenbach of Human & Rousseau Publishers graciously stepped in to salvage the enterprise; the advantage of this delay was that in 2007 Antjie and I could return to the manuscript and undertake a last comprehensive revision. Particularly with poetry, such revisions can obviously continue interminably; but at some stage a halt has to be called, for better or for worse. After much discussion, several more poems from *Escape* were relinquished, in an attempt to ensure that readers eager to discover Ingrid's work for themselves could do so without having to wade through too much inferior juvenilia which at this stage may blur rather than brighten Ingrid's image. Certainly, it is to be hoped that at some moment in the future it would be feasible to attempt a *Collected Works* (which would include also her play and her small but significant output in prose) in which justice can be done to the full extent of her contribution to South African literature.

André Brink
Cape Town, 2007

Escape (Ontvlugting, 1956)

For Abr. H. Jonker

Escape

From this Valkenburg have I run away
and in my thoughts return to Gordon's Bay:

I play with tadpoles swimming free
carve swastikas in a red-krantz tree

I am the dog that slinks from beach to beach
barks dumb-alone against the evening breeze

I am the gull that swoops in famished flights
to serve up meals of long-dead nights

The god who shaped you from the wind and dew
to find fulfilment of my pain in you:

Washed out my body lies in weed and grass
in all the places where we once did pass.

Valkenburg: mental institution in Cape Town

Puberty

The child in me died quietly
neglected, blind and quite unspoilt

subsiding slowly in a little pool
and drowning somewhere in the night

while you, in obtuse animal state,
still laughed and revelled in festivity.

In that crude way you did not foretell
that death or peril was drawing near

but in my sleep I see small hands
and in the dark your teeth's white fire:

Trembling I keep on wondering
Did you kill the child in me . . .?

At the Goodwood show

They selected me and put me on a throne
inside this prison where I live alone

round which, still free, they saunter by
and cannot understand my voiceless cry

around my neck a First Prize hangs
but in the twilight, nearly mad, I feel the pangs

of longing for the flock, remote from praise
and for the veld of the Karoo, the dust, the haze

where proud I still can stand against the evening breeze
one of the nameless horde that no-one sees,

Without the yoke of fame, without the thirst,
without upon my chest that First.

Song of the rag doll

I am the rag doll that does not speak
and your love's the only love I seek

At night I'm blind and dumb and dead
I no longer raise my bran-stuffed head

My hands don't move, my limbs go numb
And when you leave I'm stiff and dumb

Without your help I cannot walk:
you simply bought me like a dog

and you will, one Guy Fawkes night
burn me gay in festive light

I am the rag doll with no mind
My pain the loud binge of your kind.

Double game

I was amused by our double game
the nodding talk, the cheating play

One mirror in my room was
shiny-smooth, the other cracked

Perhaps you think, god-man, you fathomed me;
but I'll confuse and wound you so

that you will rush from glass to glass and ask:
if this is she, by God, who may the other be . . .?

Dedication

You be the path on which once more
I can walk barefoot on the spiky thorns
to where the ferns and arums grow
– and marigolds string garlands on the veld . . .

Wind song

Where sleeps my love, o my love in this night
stars that sway in pines and winds
stars that sway and stars that wait
o where sleeps my love, o my love in this night?

Dark pine and red path, o hear the night sing,
night song of beasts and tenebrous winds
Where sleeps my love, and who stills his pain
will I ever find him, my lost love, again?

Winter wind, guide me through bitterest nights
until from darkness I softly can stare
to see how he slumbers, and slumbering starts
to calm in my heart all the grief that I bear!

Smoke and Ochre (Rook en Oker, 1963)

For Uys Krige and Jack Cope

1

On all faces

On all faces of all people
always your eyes the two brothers
the event of yourself and the unreality
of this world

All sounds repeat your name
all buildings think it and the posters
the typewriters guess it and the sirens echo it
every birth cry confirms it and the renunciation
of this world

My days search for the vehicle of your body
my days search for the shape of your name
always before me in the path of my eyes
and my only fear is reflection
that wants to change your blood into water
that wants to change your name into a number
and to deny your eyes like a memory

Pregnant woman

Under the crust of night I lie singing,
curled up in the sewer, singing,
and my offspring lies in the water.

I play I'm a child:
gooseberries, gooseberries and heather,
kukumakrankas, aniseed,
and the tadpole slides
in the slime in the stream,
in my body
my foamwhite figure;
but sewer o sewer,
my offspring lies in the water.

Membrane red of bloodsong still singing,
I and my yesterday,
my yesterday suspended under my heart,
my kalkoentjie, my swaying world,
and my heart that sings like a cicada
my cicada heart sings like a cicada;
but sewer o sewer
my offspring lies in the water.

I play I'm happy:
look how far the firefly splashes!
the moonslice, a wet snout that quivers –
but with the morning, the limping midwife
chilly and grey on the shifting hills,
I push you out through the crust into daylight,
o grieving owl, great owl of daylight,

freed from my womb but soiled
soiled with my tears
and infected with sadness.

Sewer o sewer,
I lie shivering singing,
how else but shivering
with my offspring submerged in your water . . .?

1957

kukumakranka – red or red-and-white,
sweet-smelling wild flower (*Gethyllis ciliaris*)
kalkoentjie – red wild flower from *gladiolus* family

I repeat you

I repeat you
without beginning or end
repeat your body
The day has a thin shadow
the night yellow crosses
the landscape has no distinction
and the people a row of candles
while I repeat you
with my breasts
which imitate the hollows of your hands

I went to seek for the path of my body

I went to seek for the path of my body
and could find only strange scars in the dust
Spoor of blue wildebeest elephants and leopards
trampled over the sure secret of the white path
O I just wanted to know your shadow, small steenbok
and the slight weight of your body in flight

Autumn morning

Spear of the horizon pierces sea and sky
morning kisses on my breasts like rising suns
through all waters you will come
all forests   along all paths
in every dream that I don't remember
your hands that give themselves away
and your body that plunges into the wounded autumn

Morning sunbeams warm the room like
golden squirrels in search of hidden secrets

I searched for my own heart

I searched for my own heart
and long after I had lost my way
in the days trailing past with their foliage
in the aloof sky blue with distance
I thought I'd find my heart
where I'd kept your eyes two brown butterflies
and I saw the swallow swoop up
                        and shadows starlings

Forlorn city

In the rain that has passed
faraway day and forlorn city
of acorns   of doves full of dawn

my hands were pure squirrel
quick   furtive but ready
faraway day and forlorn city

through all the people you came
with a simple smile
as if from a long journey

and the rain that has passed
warmed itself on my body
the rain of smoke and ochre

that smells of your hands washed clean
warm doves and the open
orange poppy of the sky

Reclaimed land

I reclaimed you from the sea
and where the storm waters were
returned the earth to you

Seed of my desire   sun of my word
that plants trees in your furrows
on the coast of the dead

I curved a heaven above you
sank foundations and let a city
blossom from your earth

I returned you to the sky
but at the first sirens I
fled from you

2 Intimate conversation

Don't sleep

Don't sleep, look!
Behind the curtains the day begins to dance
with a peacock feather in its hat

When you call me

When you call me from your throat
a moist footpath opens up
in a dense wood

I know

I know of course
your mouth is a little nest
of fledgling birds

When you laugh

Your laugh is a split pomegranate
Laugh again
so I can hear how pomegranates laugh

When you were a baby

When you were a baby
you no doubt smelled
like a little billy-goat
and flowers

When you sleep

When you sleep
your forehead is a mountain
and your temples
like lambs on the slopes

Your body

Your body is
heavy with blood
and your back
a singing guitar

Every man has a head

Every man has a head
a body
and two legs
they're trying to imitate you

3

Last night

last night in your arms
by the horseshoe moon
we picked a small clover
with four leaves on

today I am standing
in the yard by the bin
my heart all mistrusting
like a chicken at a tin

picking at one grain   a stone
down the slope turning
love is nothing more
than the yearning

The troubadour's ditty

At my house or where I roam
everywhere I'm almost home

in the chamber of the night
I forget sometimes I wait for light

but the instant which escapes the yoke
from ferris wheel or casual joke

finds the coldly gleaming ways
back to where your silence stays

back to the eagle of your sight
into the blue, in lofty flight

until you drop me from your tongue
back on hard earth, unseen, unsung

Ramkiekie tune

Wherever I go no matter how far
a path runs before me
open and sharp
from my eyes like a scar

The day may turn blue
or red-plume at me
I follow my sorrow
and the signboard is you

ramkiekie – (also *ramkietjie*) 'Hottentot' guitar

Bitter-berry daybreak

Bitter-berry daybreak
bitter-berry sun
a mirror has broken
between me and him

I try to find the highway
perhaps to run away
but everywhere the footpaths
of his words lead me astray

Pinewood remember
pinewood forget
however much I lose my way
I step on my regret

Parrot-coloured echo
tricks me tricks me on
until I turn beguiled
to retrieve the mocking song

Echo gives no answer
he answers everyone
bitter-berry daybreak
bitter-berry sun

You have tricked me

You've tricked me Dolie
you've cheated me like hell
my heart o little gooseberry
has shrivelled in its shell

The pastors say   oh surely no
my mum says   go away
my granny thinks   oh heavens
our help has gone astray

But Dolie bokkie baby
you turned me down it's true
in vain I grow my little days
like chickens all for you

No matter that I offer you
a fig with day-break's tan
last night o my attatjie
you had another man

My tame owl and my mongrel
they howl through nights and days
but Dolie bokkie baby
we howl one word   always

bokkie – literally 'little buck'; term of endearment
attatjie – term of endearment: little girl

It's six of one

It's six of one my dearie
whether   Florrie Griet or Buck
half a dozen of the other
when the full-moon calls cluck-cluck

      The days fall down like sparrows
      one by one from the mottled sky
      and one by one the paths lead back
      to the same place by and by

How does the miracle compare
the birth of my own girl
it's six of one my dearie
whether Rita, Rose or Pearl

      The shadow of the nights
      hangs weary and hangs cold
      the same hearts beat in church
      or bar, in young as well as old

It's six of one my dearie
in the Congo or the Cape
the arguments may differ
but it's just the same old hate

      And six of one it stays
      whether very strange or odd
      each one is like the other
      a person before God

All too human

Now you're sad-like   Willy
but I swear   my bokkie
you're still the baby chick
in my heart's small doppie

I was far from home
and the great tent of the sky
stretched white above the road
where my footprints lie

Ag you know mos Willy
and you know my whim
to kiss a man
is to fall in love with him

And I loved him dearly
I'll not disagree
or I'd never have wanted him
for all the world to see

But that very night already
in his warm pondokkie
he was just another form
of you   my bokkie

ag – ah, oh
doppie – little house (literally: 'little shell')
mos – anyway, of course
pondokkie – little hut

On the footpath

On the footpath   o bokkie
Your hand in mine
Our little house waiting
In my heart's confine

Throughout the bee's day
till the red dusk   o bokkie
The night seals itself off
In our pondokkie

Damp of your body
o meidjie   dew-soft
Over the nevermore day
your eyes fly aloft

Already the night peels
and its brightness spills
Where the lonely footpath
runs over blue hills

meidjie – term of endearment: little (black or coloured) girl

4

Early summer
for Simone

Early summer and the sea
a quince burst open
the sky like a child's
balloon
high above the water
Under the beach-umbrellas
like striped candy
people like ants
and the generous laugh of the bay
has golden teeth

    Child with the small yellow pail
    and the forgotten pigtail
    surely your mouth is a tinkling bell
    little uvula tiny clapper
    You play the sun all day
    like a ukulele

Pixie love
for Simone

The pixie with the red-red cap
who dances to a yellow tune
he gave his heart to me last night
and his shirt went to the moon

The blue-blue sky round like a hoop
fell bumpity-bump on the ground
all shiny-blue it was rolled in his hand
a ball to throw around

The stars they winked at us as we laughed
they beamed their lights so bright
they circled us in a glittering ring
like a laager in the night

The evening flower on its trumpety-trump
blew in the whirlwind-round
kalkoentjies with their red little mouths
sang a waltz to the grasshopper sound

The moon with his yellow body
lay flat on his back on high
he fell asleep among daisies
potbelly turned to the sky

The pixie with the red-red heart
told me while dancing around
he threw the globe right over his head
for this is where love will be found

kalkoentjies – red wild flowers from *gladiolus* family

Little grain of sand

Grain little grain of sand
pebble rolled in my hand
pebble thrust in my pocket
a keepsake for a locket

Little sun big in the blue
a granule I make out of you
shine in my pebble little grain
for the moment that's all I can gain

Baby that screams from the womb
nothing is big in this tomb
quietly laugh now and speak
silence in dead-end street

Little world round and earth-blue
make a mere eye out of you
house with a door and two slits
a garden where everything fits

Small arrow feathered into space
love fades away from its place
Carpenter seals a coffin that's bought
I ready myself for the nought

Small grain of sand is my word, my breath
small grain of nought is my death

Hush now the darkling man
for Simone

On the green footpath
of the horizon far
around the earth little one,
an old man trudges who wears
an open moon in his hair
Nightingale in his heart
jasmin plucked for his buttonhole
and a back bowed down by his years.

    What's he doing, mummy?

He calls the crickets
He calls the black
silence that sings
like the rushes, my sweet
and the stars which throb
knock-knock my love,
like the tiny little beetles
in their thin far ring.

    What's his name, mummy?

His name is Hush
His name is Sleep
Mister Forget
from the Land of Dream
His name is hush
he's called, my sweet
Hush now, the darkling man

    Mummy...

Hush now, the darkling man

Ladybird
a memory of my mother

Gleaming ochre
and a light breaks
from the sea.

    In the back yard
    somewhere between the washing
    and a pomegranate tree
    your laugh and the morning
    sudden and small
    like a ladybird
    fallen on my hand

My doll falls and breaks

The shadow forewarns the street
from a high balcony flung
through the meagre jacarandas of the sky
the shadow forewarns the sun

through the song of the pennywhistles
fallen on the booming street
my doll with a name like a body
who just like us could speak

My doll shot like a sparrow
berry-naked from the window-sill stand
or was it the wind from the distance
or was it my very own hand

My doll fell down when the sun
rang its brass bell from the sky
when the clouds white-washed the walls
the shadow fell back from on high

The shadow forewarns the sun
porcelain with far sky amiss -
if I should fall from a high balcony
if I should break   would I also look like this

5

The child who was shot dead by soldiers in Nyanga

The child is not dead
the child raises his fists against his mother
who screams Africa   screams the smell
of freedom and heather
in the locations of the heart under siege

The child raises his fists against his father
in the march of the generations
who scream Africa   scream the smell
of justice and blood
in the streets of his armed pride

The child is not dead
neither at Langa nor at Nyanga
nor at Orlando nor at Sharpeville
nor at the police station in Philippi
where he lies with a bullet in his head

The child is the shadow of the soldiers
on guard with guns saracens and batons
the child is present at all meetings and legislations
the child peeps through the windows of houses and into the
                                             hearts of mothers
the child who just wanted to play in the sun at Nyanga is
                              everywhere
the child who became a man treks through all of Africa
the child who became a giant travels through the whole world

Without a pass

On the death of a virgin

I shall tell him that you have not died
He with his body like a battlefield will know this
so that his hands will forever reach for the apples of dawn
He will go out into a street without potholes
and know where to look for his heart under the newspapers
he will know where to find his heart under the mine dumps
the comrades the wine barrels and the literature of the stage
The cars will slam on their brakes and the murderers
thrust their blades back into their sheaths   the lights
will spell a small crest of yellow crosses for his crossing
The people will greet him with a sprint of hosannas
He will walk like a man in clothes without scars
His laugh will be like an ample bunch of grapes
hanging in the purple shade under the vine leaves
his smile which imitates distant roads and white gables
a harbour without warships and a sky without airfields
He will know that you have not died
your death was a matinée for children
and your body a vowel for any word

Seen from the wound in my side

I looked down from the mountains and saw I was dead
My sculpted temples   the two lambs   in the abattoirs of gold
and my hands   the crops of doves   broken with the palms
                                                turned up
O that the word which comes bleeding from my mouth
give form back to my body
and the sun the line to the hills of wheat
For the waters of my death seek the olive branches of the sun
and my people the open protea of the dawn
Above the machinery of gold the dignity of their shoulders
in the door of their homesteads   in the mouths of horses
green sunlight   with their feet dragging
But were they to meet me in the coin
of each second spinning on a counter
in the eagle heart of the night filled with maimed bodies
they would crucify me again and again   who have come to
                                                redeem them
Because I believe that there still occurs
in the outskirts of the heart
the white birth of the arum lilies
For I have seen how you   John
placed your hand on the shoulder of the black man with the cross

I do not want to receive any more visits

I do not want to receive any more visits
neither with cups of tea   nor coffee   and especially not brandy
I do not want to hear   how they're waiting   for winged letters
I do not want to hear   how they lie awake   in their eyesockets while
the others are sleeping   wide like the horizon   around his brows
and what do I want to know about their similar complaints
one without ovaries   the other with leukaemia
the child without a willy   and the old man
who has already forgotten that he's deaf
the attack of death in the traffic lights of green
the people who live by the sea as in the Sahara
the traitors of life with the face of death and of God

all I want to be is alone   travelling with my solitude
like a walking stick
and believe that I'm still unique

Bushveld

I have always lost my way
on all the footpaths, marula
You were always repeated in the circle

Singing filled with birds
Green filled with leaves
Or winter, marula

I shall always recognise you
on all the scars

marula – large tree with edible fruit (*Sclerocarya caffra*)

25 December 1960
On the death of Dylan Thomas

Ward 130 in the passage down the right.
It's five in the morning for the milk-cart
has gone by with its horses   eyes gleaming
in the bayonets of street lights.
25 December 1960.
The children sleep
in christmas stockings among satellites
hobby-horses   revolvers   and toffees.
Sleeping   before the sirens of the sun
before the bombers of the butterflies
Sleep in your christmas stockings and candles.
On Hospital Hill stands a blazing tree.
Ward 130 in the passage down to the right.
'Sure he drank a bottle of brandy
and lay for hours in an oxygen tent.
You know he was an alcoholic from
his first glass.' (Look, the day's
gleaming gun-barrel takes aim over the city!)
'Oh well, but he once said himself
he had a yearning for his dead God.
His final words? No
he just lay still, and with eyes open.'
Ward 130. He has been
attended to   eyes closed   hands already folded
the whole room like a raised shield.

And on the window sill and against the light
the mantis in unending prayer.

Based on a translation by the poet

The song of the broken reeds

The wind from the Torwana Mountains
has her lap filled with moss
She bears a sleeping child
she cites the stars
with the voice of wide waters
against the white bones of the day

The wind from the Torwana Mountains
shoreless without horizon without seasons
has the face of all people
has the aloe of the world in front of her chest
has the lamb of all joy over her shoulder
and the butcher-bird of every dawn in her eyes

The wind from the Torwana Mountains
with her lap filled with moss
bears a sleeping child
bears a night of thistles
bears a death without darkness

and blows through the broken reeds

Daisies in Namaqualand

Why do we still listen
to the answers given by the daisies
to the wind to the sun
what has become of the little kokkewiets

    Behind the closed forehead
    where perhaps a twig still tumbles
    from a drowned springtime
    Behind my word killed in action
    Behind our divided home
    Behind the heart locked against itself
    Behind wire fences, camps, locations
    Behind the silence where foreign languages
    fall like bells at a funeral
    Behind our land torn apart

sits the green mantis of the veld
and dazed we still hear
small blue Namaqualand daisy
answering something, believing something, knowing something.

kokkewiet: boubou, *Lanarius ferrugineus*

We
for André

in this way you will die off from me
like your futile seed
naked like water   a burning shimmer
like late
april
like hands   naked

lovely as mortality
as a final word
sad as blood
no little one
only
this little death

tomorrow the burning shimmer of our un-
begotten seed   tomorrow
dawn the blossoms
new girls like virgins
tomorrow
you die   and I

L'art poétique

To stow myself away like a secret
in a sleep of lambs and of cuttings
To stow myself away
in the salute of a great ship
To stow away
in the violence of a simple memory
in your drowned hands
to stow myself away in my word

Tilting Sun (Kantelson, 1966)

For Simone

Face of love
for Jack

Your face is the face of all the others
before you and after you and your eyes calm as a blue
dawn that breaks again and again
herder of the clouds
keeper of the white ever-changing beauty
the landscape of your declared mouth that I have discovered
retains the secret of a smile
like small white villages beyond the mountains
and your pulse the measure of their rapture
there is no question of beginning
there is no question of possession
there is no question of death
face that I love
the face of love

There's only one for ever

Ochre evening and your hands
a vineyard through summer and frost?
Eyes of rain over the lands, but
there's only one for ever

Instant of your luminous body,
word without language – treachery
of your gleaming hands, for
there is only one for ever

Green growth of the Inexorable
summered grown and ripened
great gleam of the ochre earth, o
there is only one for ever

Tokoloshe

We children always knew
it's devil's poison-cup you eat
we love bulbs and frutang
but all and sundry greet

their own dear love. In the bush
one plays with water one with clay
till noontime when the red-breast
and the sun curve out the day

then we don't see your wrinkles
nor your laughter's trace
then scared of things that grab
we see the dark side of your face

Scared of taunting scared of scorn
we scuttle from the bush
we children knew mos all along
what they call Love is tokoloshe

mos – of course
tokoloshe – African hobgoblin, often with sexual connotations
frutang – wild fruit (Rumulea rosea)

O the half-moon

O the half-moon is the slice of day
that floats forgotten in the high black sky
but I feel the climate of your body today
Say again say again say again

and I unfold like a star in your hips
and your body dips hotly into mine
till the night runs far away from its tracks
Farewell farewell farewell

sound of your eyes rhythm of your chest
Wound of your hands your thighs o thirst
of your lips the night breaks its crust
Forget forget forget

Song of the grave digger

Where gaunt cypresses keep their watch
among the corpses of yesterday
I have to dig two new graves
and like a poet while time away

shall I ponder the way the soul escapes
and how the procession here will stand
and bury their dead friend and then
in need of him go home again

and in modern vein I'll think
how my life lies in the dust
and after that to cheer me up
sing to myself a song of praise

but every day I shall remember
how you departed from my house
among the graves I feel myself
today and daily more at home

here where gaunt cypresses keep their watch
I buried you as well my child
With neither prayer nor grave nor sigh
just the winter wind and I

Conversation on a hotel terrace

My death throbs behind my eyeballs like the moon
I hear it move behind the peals of waves
I measure its progress in the slime-track of a snail
The days fall like sparrows into the earth
And every word has the appearance of Nothingness

We, on the open terrace, count the jubilation of the stars
When you laugh the rhythmic path of workers breaks open
                                                      in my veins

I measure the act of your eyes the horizons
I hear the day steal by like a child full of secrets
And were you to ask what I'm always thinking of I'd answer
Child, a small rambling rose, or a glass of water

Drawing
for Jack

You whom I draw with a pencil
like one's own secret
a letter a phone number
You whom I draw with a pencil
like a child a naked stick man
under his desk at school
You whom I draw with a pencil
a word a name a cadence
I have journeyed through like blood
family circles laws battlefields
like desolation the eyes
of the world
You whom I draw with a pencil
scant lines trembling insecure
secret beyond the secret of veins
secret far beyond love

Walk

The day, the pale hand-shaker
is outside at the window
I am not scared of him!
But look at his ugly face!
This morning I'll walk in my little garden
I and my mongrel dog
I'll pick a rose for my house
I'll rake the ground
I am not scared of you!
I'll not think of you
I've done nothing to you
The hurt in your eyes?
It is your own fault!
I am not scared of you!
You jerk me from my sleep
with every new morning
that yawns outside my window
Have you no decency then?

You come just like the light
and flash your wounded eye
right in my face!
You should be ashamed!
Yes I too was a child
the sun my red marble
o who won it from me
on which track, where is the place . . .

Come doggy, you are falling behind!

Dark stream

Green stream full of life
in which the sun gazes
I cannot speak with you
you have too many secrets
Shall I speak to the little tadpoles?
They are too timid.
Tell them they'll become big frogs?
That's too uncertain.
Shall I cry because one of them sinks
before his back legs are out?
That's too unimportant.
Stream in which the dark
sees nothing but the dark
with you I can speak
I know you better.

On the road to death

On the road to death strides your name, Christ.
The heart of your eyes throbs on the lips of children.
The figure of your word lies in the sighs of lovers
up to the last folds of joy amen.

Revelation, meaning, bone and marrow, language;
Pronouncer of the dream, interpreter of the Almighty,
in your eyes I have seen eternity without distance
I have descended to the ultimate sounding boards of God.

Master, at the temple veil of dawn
with my own death on my tongue I give you back
to life, with my bloodstained name, mocked,
crucified, the very verb of love, Judas Iscariot.

Dog

I lie under your hand – a mongrel
in the growling silence
in the yelping moonlight
latticed among stars, she
in her terrible
white comes and goes.

(I also longed to go hunting hares
over my own karoo
over my burning plains
from ochre to ochre,   o
white plains of your hands!)

Tonight I shall bare my teeth
and tear at the wily rhythm of the moon
listen to my innocence and distance
my long resounding bark
from my kennel; white moon, white baas,
in the night.

baas – master

I lament you

I lament your blurred body
blue as your eyes blurred and wide the sea
My hand of dust
cannot protect you
can barely alter the road
on which your despondent footsteps
must settle in seaweed
My hand of dust
cannot brave the rocks

But the seagulls can.

30/1/1965

The morning is you

The air is filled with roses
the roses are defenceless
defenceless your hands your eyes
rose of your mouth
the morning is you
defenceless rose of the morning
wound of the roses

Old man travelling

I often saw an old man
peacefully travelling without hope
of the stop that signals with its lights
like the luminous cross of death

Two hearts

Two hearts I have
the one pumps blood
and the other really looks like
an appeliefkosie
or a paddatjie

appeliefkosie – a combination of the words *appeliefie* (Cape gooseberry) and *appelkosie* (small apricot): in addition, *liefkoos* means to caress
paddatjie – little frog; is also a child's word for a little girl's sex

How long will it last

How long will it last
moment of reality
without the madness
and in touch with the dream?

3/5/1963

All that breaks

All that breaks, falls or ends
– like the ejaculation of seed–
has no other significance
than betrayal.

Because everything shaped, completed or begun
– like life begotten in the womb –
has no other fulfilment
than the tomb.

My embrace redoubled me
for André

My embrace redoubled me

my breasts call to each other
the two prancing friends
and my hands enclose my secrets

in a room far away

behind the spilled autumn
your eyes gaze astounded
at the mirror of your body

Lullaby for the beloved

Tula tula
your little body rolled
your little lamb sleeps
deep in his wool
tula tula

September 1964

tula (Xhosa) – be still, be quiet

When you write again
for Jack

When you write again in your diary
Remember
To see the golden leaf in the summer sun
Or perhaps the blue moederkappie
On one of our absentminded rambles
On Table Mountain
I who mingled my blood with the blood of
The evening sun in Lisbon
Carried you with me like a mirror
And I have written you
On the open page
Of my sadness
Your nameless word
When you write again in your diary
Remember
To see in my eyes
The sun that I now cover for ever
With black butterflies

moederkappie – small terrestrial orchid (Disperis capensis); literally 'mother's bonnet'

Waiting in Amsterdam
for André
for Jack

I can only say that I waited for you
through western nights
at tram stops
in lanes
by canals
and the tower of tears

You came
through the forlorn cities of Europe
I recognised you
I prepared the table
with wine with bread with grace
but unperturbed you turned your back
you took off your cock
laid it on the table
and without a word
with your own smile
forsook the world

Journey around the world for André

Olive journeys
trees   water
you with your body of ferns
dreaming in my arms close by the Seine
with your body
of white gables
with your body
of bitter sun
in Barcelona
(behind the bullfights
the siestas of your eyes)
Journeys of silence
journeys of walls
journeys of marble
couplets of small
hard
words
pass away
but you
dreaming in water ferns and sun
in my arms close by the Seine
go forth
impregnate the earth

Your name has a dinky car
for André

Your name has a dinky car
your name has a boyish smile
and a sudden small puddle

What will the auctioneer use for your name?

Your name which I call through the dark
Be warned!

For you are being sold
at a public auction
blindfolded
to the bourgeoisie

You're being sold
my virginal word

like an

old

horse

4/9/1963

Nostalgia for Cape Town

She shelters me within the multitudes of her lap
She says my throat will not be cut
She says I'm not being put under house arrest
She says I'm not dying of the galloping consumption of love
She doesn't know I'm hungry
She doesn't know I'm scared
She doesn't know that the cock-crow and the house arrest
                                        are mating
I am her enfant terrible
With cups of tea she keeps Table Mountain at bay
And her hands are cool as spoons

July 1964

Plant me a tree André

plant me an oak tree
so that I can recognise my shape
and the squirrels can bury their acorns there

give me a dog
with paws I can kiss
at night while you sleep wrathful and well

don't let them chop down my tree
uproot revile or splinter it
grant it a heaven with acres of blue acorns

make me an open house
so that my windows may discover the day
green or gold or grey but well-shaped

grant that my dog may love me
that I may give him food to stuff himself
while you sleep beyond the stars and mirrors

of my forehead

26/12/1964

This journey
for Jack

This journey which obliterates your shape
torn blood-angel thrown to the dogs
this landscape is deserted as my forehead
Wound of the roses

How I longed to see you walk without chains
how I longed to see again your open face
face broken and dead as the mud
Wound of the mud

In the nights of absence without eyes
I wished to see a genuine star in your hand
I wished to see the blue sky blue and to hear
a single human word

Bitter angel untrue with a flame in your mouth
under your armpits I will place two swallows
and draw a secret cross over your body
For the man

of whom you once reminded me.

(Based on a translation by the poet)

Mommy

mommy is no longer a person
just an a
she gets dressed
she goes to the hairdresser
she walks in the streets
her feet trip
she consults the psychiatrist
just like an ordinary person

she whispers words
mon chéri
it has no sound
it's the white
whispering of a ghost
it has no colour
and it bolts
it giggles from lifts
it peers through spectacles
it wonders on the sly
it is disarmed
it is naked as an african
it would like to believe in people
never mind a god

15/7/1964

Waterfall of moss and sun
for André

Moss waterfall
tilting sun
I
love
you
Moss waterfall
tilting sun
thief of
my heart
thief
moss waterfall
tilting sun
Falling
fall
fall
Fast
fast
fin
In the small pool
tiny pebble
little rings of water
clarity

You

my own
face

4/2/1964

I am with those

I am with those
who abuse sex
because the individual doesn't count
with those who get drunk
against the abyss of the brain
against the illusion that life
once was beautiful or good or significant
against the garden parties of pretence
against the silence beating at the temples
with those who poor and old
compete against death the atom bomb of days
with those numbed in institutions
shocked with electric currents
through the cataracts of nerves
with those who have been deprived of their hearts
like colour from the traffic light of safety
with those coloureds africans dispossessed
with those who kill
because every death confirms anew
the lie of life
and please forget
about justice   it doesn't exist
about brotherhood   it's a fraud
about love   it has no right

January 1965

(Based on the original English version by the poet, March 1964)

I drift in the wind
for Anna

Loose I have my own independence
from graves from treacherous friends
the hearth I have comforted glowers at me
my parents have broken themselves off from my death
the worms stir against my mother, my father
clasps his hand which feathers loose against the sky
loose I believe my old friend has forsaken me
loose I believe you have toppled mountains in me
loosened my landscape reeks of bitter sun and blood

What will become of me
the cornerstones of my heart bring about nothing
my landscape is mine hardened
fierce embittered but open
My volk,
follow my lonely fingers
people, wrap yourselves in generosity
veiled by the sun of the future
My black Africa
follow my lonely fingers
follow my absent image
lonely as an owl
and the lonesomest fingers of the world
lonesome as my sister
My volk has rotted away from me
what will become of this rotted volk
a hand cannot pray on its own

The sun shall be covered by us
the sun in our eyes for ever covered
with black butterflies

volk – nation, with specific ethnic (Afrikaner) connotations